AF734894

Jennifer Williamson is a Partner at Blake Morgan LLP, based in the firm's Southampton office but regularly working from other locations including London and Oxford. She specialises in family law, undertaking a full range of divorce, financial remedy, and private Children Act work in which she acts for a wide and varied client base.

Jennifer regularly features in the legal directories (Legal 500, Chambers and Partners) where she is ranked as a "Next Generation Partner" and "Up & Coming". The flowing published testimonials evidence the high regard for her from clients and fellow practitioners alike. Her technical expertise, proportionate and human approach are particularly noted.

Jennifer has been at the forefront of thought leadership about the interplay between menopause and family law. She is passionate about the need for recognition of, and a sensible, balanced approach to, the issues.

A Practical Guide to Menopause and Family Law

A Practical Guide to Menopause and Family Law

Jennifer Williamson

Law Brief Publishing

Published 2023 by Law Brief Publishing, an imprint of Law Brief Publishing Ltd
30 The Parks
Minehead
Somerset
TA24 8BT

www.lawbriefpublishing.com

Paperback: 978-1-912687-63-3

PREFACE

Family lawyers work hard to keep up to date with the ever changing social and legal landscape in which they work. A significant increase in societal recognition and interest about how the menopause affects people has not passed us by. Articles, projects and seminars have made great strides in terms of helping practitioners start to connect menopausal symptoms and the legal work they are undertaking for clients. This book brings together a lot of this information and thought leadership, and adds a very practical slant to make it more easily applicable to cases.

I would take this opportunity to thank Imogen Robins, of Pump Court Chambers, for allowing me to share the stage with her at recent seminars addressing menopause and family law.

Any author royalties raised by this book will be donated to a menopause charity of the author's choice.

The stated law in this book is believed to be correct and up to date as at 17 March 2023.

Jennifer Williamson
March 2023

CONTENTS

Chapter One	Why This Is Important	1
Chapter Two	Relationship Breakdown	13
Chapter Three	Approach & Path	17
Chapter Four	Financial Remedy Work	25
Chapter Five	Nuptial Agreements	43
Chapter Six	Children Act 1989 Matters	47
Chapter Seven	Domestic Abuse & Family Law Act Applications	53
Chapter Eight	Cohabitation Matters	59
Chapter Nine	Disability, Protected Characteristics, Ethnic Minorities, Ethnic Groups and LGBTQ+	61
Chapter Ten	Evidence and Experts	63
Chapter Eleven	Should the Menopause Be Run as an Issue?	69

Chapter Twelve	Family Lawyers and the Menopause	73
Chapter Thirteen	Avoiding Potential Negligence	77
Conclusion		79

CHAPTER ONE

WHY THIS IS IMPORTANT

The last few years have seen family law, and wider communities increasingly recognise how the menopause can adversely impact a person's ability to live and work as normal. This has been widely received as a welcome and important development in equity.

Though the political treatment of this issue is beyond the remit of this book, it is also relevant to note that sustained media and press coverage of how the symptoms of menopause can affect individuals, business and the economy has pushed this issue up the political agenda. Key reports which have flowed from this include the House of Commons Women and Equalities Committee on Menopause and the workplace report of 28 July 2022. The Government's response was published on 24 January 2023 which accepted around half of the recommendations in full, part and in principle but notably decided against making the menopause a protected characteristic under the Equality Act and against the introduction of "menopause leave" pilots in England.

The spotlight on menopause within family law cases is possibly more recent and at the time of writing this text there are **no** reported cases in which the family court has made a particular decision because of the menopause and/or where a decision has been influenced by a party experiencing menopausal symptoms.

Family lawyers may be aware of a number of employment tribunal cases concerned with menopause discrimination across three protected characteristics: age, sex and disability discrimination. Thus far, the employment tribunals have decided that menopause itself is not a disability but that menopausal symptoms can be disabling when the symptoms' impact on day-to-day activities is more than minor or trivial. It is, though, yet to be seen whether individuals will start to cite the menopause as a factor which the court should consider in family law cases. There is still more uncertainty about how the court might deal with such arguments as and when they arise. Though this book includes information about how such arguments could be put together and progressed, it is specifically not within its remit to predict how, when or where family law could or should develop in relation to the menopause.

What is clear at this stage is that every client who is, or might be, experiencing menopausal symptoms will have different particular needs of relevance to the running of the case if not the ultimate outcome. The purpose of this book is to identify those needs and guide practitioners to meet them.

Understand your client

The work of lawyers includes advising people about legal processes and principles. Many disciplines can do that within quite clinical and theoretical parameters. Family law is quite the opposite though, dealing with people, human relationships and conditions, an ever-changing and very individual landscape. To do this well, we need to understand our clients and their particular circumstances. It is not suggested that the need to understand your client is anything new!

What may be new, however, is specific attention now being focused upon how adverse menopausal symptoms can make it harder for people to deal with the process of divorce and other family law matters. So, at the most basic level it should assist the practitioner to know (or, perhaps more practically, have in mind) if their client, or indeed the other party in a case, might be living with such symptoms in order to help them proceed and advise accordingly.

In the first instance, to understand the particular family law issues and needs arising from the menopause, family lawyers need a basic knowledge of what the menopause is and how it can manifest itself.

What is menopause?

Menopause is when a person has stopped menstruating due to lower hormone levels, and has not menstruated for 12 months, which state usually occurs between the ages of 45 and 55[1]. Many people experience symptoms in the years before their menopause, which time is known as "perimenopause". Strictly speaking, references within this book to “the menopause” and "menopausal symptoms" are to "the perimenopause", and "perimenopausal symptoms".

This natural life event hasn't previously found itself at the centre of many discussions, particularly in the workplace or legal cases. It might even have been considered somewhat taboo. The last few years have seen people increasingly willing to speak up about their experiences, though, which has shown us that the impact on day-to-day life, relationships and work can be significant.

1 https://www.nhs.uk/conditions/menopause/

Symptoms

The NHS[2] tells us that the symptoms of menopause can last for months or years and include, at various levels of severity:

- Change to normal pattern of menstruation (periods), trend towards irregular periods and eventual cessation;
- Changes to mood: low mood, anxiety, mood swings, low self-esteem.
- Problems with memory or concentration (brain fog)
- Physical symptoms:
    - Hot flushes and dizziness
    - Difficulty sleeping: increased tiredness and irritability
    - Heart palpitations
    - Worsening headaches and migraines
    - Muscle aches and joint pains
    - Changed body shape and weight gain
    - Skin changes to include dry and itchy skin
    - Reduced libido
    - Recurrent Urinary Tract Infections

2 https://www.nhs.uk/conditions/menopause/symptoms/

Quite aside from the emotional difficulties arising from relationship breakdown, family law matters can be complex, generally requiring the people involved to provide lots of documentation, to recall and give detailed instructions sometimes including about fairly historical matters. Clients need to absorb, process and understand relatively complicated legal advice. This can be time consuming and confusing at the best of times, but very much more difficult against a backdrop of menopause symptoms as above.

Clients may be unaware, or may not acknowledge that they are experiencing menopausal symptoms. For example, they may dismiss fatigue on the basis that it is expected tiredness and exhaustion arising from the daily juggle, or the anxiety of a failing relationship. It is not for a practitioner to diagnose whether or not any particular client is experiencing the menopause. In fact, from a family law perspective invariably the relevance, and thus focus, is likely to be on the symptoms rather than cause. As such, there is a need to appropriately encourage clients to be open about their symptoms, so that we can support them by signposting to the various resources available including to GPs and other menopause specialist clinicians. A sensitive approach is inevitably required. It is unlikely that any person will want 'different treatment'. Though menopause is a natural biological life stage for most, it should not be forgotten or overlooked that some people encounter it much earlier than might be expected (for example, following a hysterectomy). Various people will experience and view things differently. There will be a broad range in terms of the level of the client's comfort discussing this topic with professional advisers.

Vulnerability

Menopausal family law clients are likely to be simultaneously dealing with relationship breakdown, taking legal advice, and symptoms of the menopause in addition to the usual trials and tribulations of day-to-day life. Balancing this number of competing, and arguably equally important, factors can make our clients *vulnerable.* The writer would suggest that it is important to recognise this and to consider that, for example, difficulties arising these factors from could contribute to people giving instructions to agree potentially detrimental terms, or they may find it more challenging to understand relatively complicated legal and financial advice. Perhaps, therefore, currently the greatest significance of menopause in family law relates to the professional client care that we provide.

Vulnerability and running a case

Before turning one's mind to how menopausal symptoms might be relevant to the legal subject matter of any particular case type, it is vital to consider the extent to which your client may be vulnerable. For the avoidance of doubt, a client's capacity to instruct is a separate issue (beyond the remit of this book) which should be considered in all cases and it is not suggested that the menopause reduces mental capacity.

Unless acknowledged and addressed, vulnerability can put clients at a disadvantage. Arguably, failing to address that disadvantage could amount to (a) not acting in the best interests of the client[3] and (b) not taking account of your client's attributes, needs and circumstances[4].

---

3 SRA Principle 7: https://www.sra.org.uk/solicitors/standards-regulations/principles/

4 Para 3.4 SRA Code of Conduct: https://www.sra.org.uk/solicitors/standards-regulations/code-conduct-solicitors/

Either would be a breach of the SRA code or principles which would bring with it the risk of a complaint to the SRA, reputational risk and financial claims for damages or compensation.

The SRA practice note[5], "Accepting instructions from vulnerable clients or third parties acting on their behalf", is a good starting point when thinking about from which reasonable adjustments, or practical support, a menopausal client may benefit. Detail of more relevance to menopausal clients is then found within The Law Society's practice note, "Meeting the needs of vulnerable clients"[6] which specifies that:

> "Living with a disability, illness or diagnosis does not in itself make someone vulnerable. In the context of legal advice, it is the person's situation and barriers to accessing legal services that may make them vulnerable. Equally, a person may be vulnerable without any disability, illness or diagnosis: for example, if they are recently bereaved or frail".

As such, many family law clients will be at risk of circumstantial vulnerability by virtue of the loss of a significant relationship, or the stress of dealing with that. Menopausal clients may be at additional risk of further vulnerability on top of that if their symptoms make it harder to access, understand and retain legal advice. A client's vulnerability may change as a matter progresses so notes should be recorded on files at the beginning, and during the lifetime of, a case to evidence the practitioner's identification of risk factors and how they have dealt with them.

---

5 https://www.sra.org.uk/solicitors/guidance/accepting-instructions-vulnerable-clients/

6 https://www.lawsociety.org.uk/topics/client-care/meeting-the-needs-of-vulnerable-clients

Dealing with vulnerability

Communication preferences

How the practitioner communicates with all clients, but particularly with those who are vulnerable, is key. Clear family law advice is more important than ever when dealing with menopause related issues within family law cases.

Paragraph 3.4[7] of the SRA's code of conduct for solicitors requires practitioners to:

> "..take account of your client's attributes, needs and circumstances..."

Moreover, paragraph 8.6 of the SRA's code of conduct for solicitors requires solicitors to:

> "..give clients information in a way they can understand..."

Particular attention should therefore be given to when and how to communicate legal advice if a client's adverse menopausal symptoms include problems with memory or concentration. Long and verbose correspondence should be avoided more than ever.

Clients should be asked about any specific needs or preferences in this regard. These may include for documents to be written in clear, simple language (as is likely to be standard for most lawyers) and/or for advice and information to be predominantly verbal. Practitioners may choose to, for example, send copies of file notes recording any key conversations and advice to the client as a matter of course. That not

---

7 SRA | Code of Conduct for Solicitors, RELs and RFLs | Solicitors Regulation Authority: https://www.sra.org.uk/solicitors/standards-regulations/code-conduct-solicitors/

only protects the lawyer, but gives the client a written record of advice to which they can refer as required.

The potential impact of vulnerability arising from adverse physical symptoms can be eased by giving due care and attention to what is the right environment in which to conduct meetings[8]. Where practitioners have the choice of meeting room, it would be sensible to select one where there is the ability to vary temperature and lighting levels. Easy access to toilet facilities, with free sanitary products, can also be helpful. Frequent breaks, refreshments and water probably all go without saying.

In the same way that we would not hesitate to specifically invite other vulnerable clients to bring a trusted friend or family member to meetings with them, this is just as pertinent and relevant to a menopausal client.

Vulnerability within court proceedings

Vulnerability should also be considered with specific reference to court proceedings. In this regard, the High Court and Court of Appeal[9] have given particular and recent guidance on special measures for vulnerable witnesses, which in a nutshell are to ensure the quality of a person's evidence is not reduced because of their vulnerability.

Part 3A of the Family Procedure Rules 2010 contains the provisions for "Vulnerable persons: participation in proceedings and giving

---

8 Equal Treatment Bench Book: https://www.judiciary.uk/about-the-judiciary/diversity/equal-treatment-bench-book/

9 Re S (Vulnerable Party: Fairness of Proceedings) [2022] EWCA Civ 8 (Lord Justice Baker, 28 January 2022; K v L and another [2021] EWHC 3225 (Fam) Mrs Justice Judd, 1 December 2021 and GK v PR [2021] EWFC 106 Mr Justice Peel 14 December 2021

evidence". Where matters are in proceedings, the court has a positive duty to consider whether a party's participation in proceedings is likely to be diminished by reason of vulnerability[10] . The court is, of course, reliant on a party, or their legal representative, to provide information about vulnerability to enable the court to conduct this exercise. Naturally, consideration about the need for this will be dealt with on a case-by-case basis. It, may, however, be helpful to bear in mind that the factors the court should consider in this regard are rather different from everything we have looked at so far, as follows:

> "(a) the impact of any actual or perceived intimidation, including any behaviour towards the party or witness on the part of—
>
> (i) any other party or other witness to the proceedings or members of the family or associates of that other party or other witness; or
>
> (ii) any members of the family of the party or witness;
>
> (b) whether the party or witness—
>
> (i) suffers from mental disorder or otherwise has a significant impairment of intelligence or social functioning;
>
> (ii) has a physical disability or suffers from a physical disorder; or
>
> (iii) is undergoing medical treatment;

---

10 3A.4 PART 3A – VULNERABLE PERSONS: PARTICIPATION IN PROCEEDINGS AND GIVING EVIDENCE (justice.gov.uk)

(c) the nature and extent of the information before the court;

(d) the issues arising in the proceedings including (but not limited to) any concerns arising in relation to abuse;

(e) whether a matter is contentious;

(f) the age, maturity and understanding of the party or witness;

(g) the social and cultural background and ethnic origins of the party or witness;

(h) the domestic circumstances and religious beliefs of the party or witness;

(i) any questions which the court is putting or causing to be put to a witness in accordance with section 31G(6) of the 1984 Act;

(j) any characteristic of the party or witness which is relevant to the participation direction which may be made;

(k) whether any measure is available to the court;

(l) the costs of any available measure; and

(m) any other matter set out in Practice Direction 3AA."

Of these factors, paragraph (b) is likely to be most relevant to menopausal clients' evidence. It will be for the lawyer to consider with their clients whether or not symptoms are such that information needs to be given to the court to ensure vulnerability is properly taken into account.

CHAPTER TWO

RELATIONSHIP BREAKDOWN

Menopause and divorce are increasingly concurrent

In the last couple of years, the 'average' age of divorce[11] has directly converged with the 'average' age of menopause. It would also seem that women are issuing significantly more than half of divorce proceedings. Overall, it therefore seems that more than one third of

---

[11] Divorce – Office for National Statistics (ons.gov.uk): https://www.ons.gov.uk/peoplepopulationandcommunity/birthsdeathsandmarriages/divorce

Average age of women at divorce has been increasing: now 45 (within range of menopause onset). 2019: 107,599 opposite sex divorces. ONS have age information about 65,105 of them: 26,672 involved women of menopause age (45 – 55), this equates to 41%.

107,599 divorces in 2019: 66,986 were issued by women (62%)

Statistics for same-sex divorce only available 2015 – 2019 during which time mean age of a woman in a same-sex divorce has increased from 37 to nearly 40 years old.

In the last few years, for the first time, the Office for National Statistics (ONS) reported that the mean age of women at divorce has crept up to 45.3, which coincides with the generally accepted start of menopause.

Analysis: Women seem to be issuing significantly more than half of divorce proceedings and more than one third of all divorce proceedings seem to involve women of menopause age.

all divorce proceedings in England and Wales involve menopausal women. Consequently, this is far from being an unusual or little encountered set of circumstances. That factor, and the increased visibility of menopause in the wider world, means that family lawyers increasingly recognise the need to equip themselves with knowledge and information about the menopause and how this relates to their work.

Albeit to comment on the relative proportions or percentages would be entirely speculative, common sense dictates that adverse menopausal symptoms will play their own part in contributing to some relationship break downs. Whilst divorce petitions no longer state the reason for a divorce, those who were in practice for any significant time before April 2022 are likely to recall many a petition which has at least hinted at a party's lack of libido being problematic. In terms of physical symptoms, that and vaginal atrophy are menopausal symptoms which obviously might impact intimate relationships. Consequently, in some cases, the extent of symptoms themselves may lead to divorce and/or other relationship breakdown.

Perfect storm

Dealing with relationship change and menopause simultaneously is not new. Better understanding how the events interrelate will enable us all to better support our clients to achieve the outcomes they deserve, and their need to start afresh.

At the onset of the menopause, around 45 years, individuals could well be simultaneously:

- Caring for primary school age children and *either* reaching the end of a family related work or career break *or* juggling their family's ever increasing and complicated timetables, while continuing to deliver results in demanding careers.

- Considering a gear shift in terms of work, to re-ignite their career or consider promotion to a senior level.
- Starting to assume greater care responsibilities for parents or in-laws, who may be tending towards less active/healthy retirement years.
- Starting to experience the onset or increase of physical and / or psychological menopause symptoms as described above.

Though beyond the remit of this publication, it is notable that in later life, those who have gone through menopause are statistically twice as likely to be diagnosed with Alzheimer's and other forms of dementia than those people who have not gone through menopause. This in turn can often have financial implications in terms of the cost of end-of-life care needs.

CHAPTER THREE

APPROACH & PATH

As above, the challenges of any relationship change will be *in addition* to menopausal symptoms. Clients with this profile may well be vulnerable and have additional needs.

At the outset of any type of family law case, having considered vulnerability, the family law practitioner will be thinking about strategy and approach. Where there are any flags which may suggest the client is within the perimenopause, the following approach can be adopted:

1. At or following the first meeting with your client, consider and record on the file whether there are any flags that either party may be within the perimenopause. For longer matters, keep this under review.

2. If you are acting for a client who you suspect may be, or who has confirmed they are, menopausal, talk to them to understand how the symptoms are impacting upon their day-to-day lives, and how they might impact on their ability to give instructions and receive advice. Agree with your client how you will deliver advice. For the benefit of your file, clearly record this step so there is evidence that you have considered how to deal with this vulnerability.

3. Take appropriate steps to mitigate the impact of physical symptoms during meetings.

4. Consider how menopausal symptoms might impact on the range of approaches which the client might sensibly consider

taking to resolve the legal matter. Ensure clients are fully advised about the different approaches which can be taken since the right approach may be proportionately more important than ever in a case of this nature.

The benefits and disadvantages of a range of common approaches are set out in the below table. Please note this table is limited to the impact of menopausal symptoms, but it is of course the case that there are many other factors to consider which are beyond the remit of this book.

Approach	**Benefits**	**Disadvantages**
Direct discussions between the parties without involving professionals.	• Flexible as to day, time, location. Discussions can be had at short notice to take advantage of less symptomatic times. • Ability to adjust surroundings to ensure maximum comfort;	• Vulnerable clients may be at risk of power imbalance; • Potential for unmanaged difficulties with objectivity arising from mood swings; • Evidential problems/lack of certainty if a party has significant problems with memory or concentration.
Mediation	• If remote: ability to adjust surroundings to ensure maximum comfort; • Impartial mediator likely to identify and re-focus discussions where objectivity wanders; • Mediator's notes of each session will assist those suffering with poor memory.	• Clients experiencing low self-esteem may not feel confident to attend mediation alone. • Differences between the parties' self-esteem levels could give rise to an imbalance in negotiating ability/power to the disadvantage of the menopausal party.

		• Clients with brain fog may struggle to retain and apply the legal advice taken between sessions to the discussions in mediation;
Hybrid mediation, or Collaborative approach	• Presence of solicitors can smooth transition between legal advice and negotiations; • Presence of solicitor can off-set any imbalance in negotiating ability/power by effectively lending self-esteem/ encouragement to the menopausal client during meetings. • Process more likely to involve other specialists such as a family consultant who might provide particular support with regard to menopausal mental health symptoms	• Potentially less likely to be a remote process, thus potential inability to adjust physical environment to suit; • Process involving larger number of people could increase anxiety;
Non-collaborative, solicitor-led negotiations	• Meetings limited to being with own solicitor, which may be to the benefit of controllability of physical environment and anxiety • Communications/negotiations with former partner handled by the solicitors, which again may be beneficial with regard to anxiety	• Potential for uncertainty and anxiety to arise as a result of less hands-on involvement; • Less structure can introduce drift and delay, which could be particularly unhelpful where a party has memory problems;

	• Everything fully recorded	• Process less likely to involve other professionals who can assist with non-legal aspects of menopausal symptoms.
Arbitration	• Bespoke proceedings which can take account of preferences and needs with regard to physical surroundings; • Contrasted with court proceedings, greater potential to limit evidence to written statements which may be particularly beneficial if the menopausal client may struggle to give their best evidence orally. • Potential for involvement of other therapeutic professionals to be involved; • Parties represented by solicitor/barrister which can reduce anxiety • Full record	• Decision in hands of arbitrator rather than parties, thus can increase anxiety • Potential need to give oral evidence: very likely to be difficult for party suffering from memory problems, anxiety, mood difficulties and/or low self-esteem. Concern may arise as to how physical symptoms, such as hot flush, may adversely impact on perceived quality of evidence.
Court process	• Parties represented by solicitor/barrister which can reduce anxiety	• All decisions about proceedings and outcome in hands of court, rather than parties. High likelihood of increasing anxiety.

	• Full record • Burden of making decisions lifted, which may alleviate anxiety.	• Long delays lead to increased anxiety and difficulties where memory problems exist. • Litigious process likely to heighten emotions and reduce objectivity

Support

Menopause specific support is not the role of the family lawyer. Lawyers should consider referring their clients to their own GP or a menopause specialist GP or clinic as appropriate[12] at an early stage in the matter.

How to approach the conversation

Most family lawyers have considerable experience of sensitively and tactfully asking difficult questions. We are used to routinely asking people about financial matters – the amount in their bank account, the number of credit cards they might have, how much they spend each month. We feel professionally comfortable seeking instructions about difficulties such as alcohol dependency, drug addiction, the use of prostitutes and gambling habits. Clients also sometimes unilaterally provide intimate information, such as about parties' sexual relationships, without us asking them to do so. We take this all in our stride.

Notwithstanding this, it is acknowledged that asking our clients questions about the menopause and symptoms may feel daunting to some, if not many family lawyers. There may or may not be a difference between comfort levels in this regard between practitioners.

12 https://thebms.org.uk/menopause-specialists/overview/

Foreseeably, those people who will or have experienced menopause may feel happier making enquiries of this nature, than those who will or have not. From the other perspective, as already noted, some clients will be more open to talking about menopause and symptoms than others.

In the first instance, it is important to note that lawyers do not, and indeed probably should not, need to start a conversation of this nature by asking "are you in the menopause". It is suggested that the best way forward is likely to be a series of questions (including a range of interest based, exploratory, open and focussed questions) with the aim of yielding information about symptoms, as opposed to the menopause per se.

Practitioners may wish to consider using some or all of the below example questions to support their discussions:

1. How are you feeling?

2. Putting this legal matter aside, how are you feeling?

3. Have you noticed any changes to your mood or in your self-esteem? Can you describe those.

4. Have you been experiencing any difficulties with concentration/other symptoms other than because of the stress of this matter? Can you tell me about that?

5. What else are you going through, apart from this legal matter?

6. What sort of medical or well-being issues are you currently thinking about? What are your thoughts about how to address those?

7. How is your self-esteem? What do you think might change/improve/impact that?

8. How is your memory and concentration at the moment?

9. Has there been any change in how you feel you can concentrate or remember things? Do you have any strong preferences about receiving written or verbal advice?

10. Have you noticed any differences in how you react to people and situations?

11. Are you worried about any matters relating to your health?

12. Can you tell me a little bit about your mood?

13. Could you describe what happens when you feel anxious? How long have you felt like that? Do you think this is having any impact on the decisions you are making?

14. How are you sleeping? For how long have you been sleeping badly?

15. Do you think anything other than these legal matters may be adversely impacting the quality of your sleep?

16. Have you noticed how any of these symptoms vary or not in terms of severity?

17. How do the symptoms you have described impact on how you feel about this matter? Can you tell me about how your symptoms have made any difference to your confidence?

18. Have you spoken to anybody about how you are feeling?

19. Have you taken advice from your GP?

20. How are you dealing with your symptoms? What medication have you been offered and/or are you taking?

21. Is there anything interfering with your usual ability to make clear decisions?

22. Are there any health issues, or natural life events, which might affect your ability to take part in and progress this matter?

Additionally, as with any sensitive discussion, thought should be given to the tone and approach likely to maximise the prospects of it going well. At the risk of stating the obvious, lawyers should think about:

- Establish trust and rapport by discussing 'easier' ground first;

- Make and maintain appropriate eye contact;

- Promoting a relaxed dialogue;

- Try not to rehearse the content of the conversation in advance: this can lead to the lawyer attempting to 'fill in the gaps' to the detriment of the quality of instructions.

- Listen: don't answer your own questions, give the client time and space to respond even if that includes allowing some time for silence;

- Positive body language: physical behaviour, expressions and mannerisms are all nonverbal communication which may reveal how you, the practitioner, feels about the conversation.

CHAPTER FOUR

FINANCIAL REMEDY WORK

Again, beyond the remit of this book, but noteworthy is that statistically, one in ten women[13] have left work because of adverse menopause symptoms, which will give rise to difficult financial circumstances for those individuals (contributing to the so-called gender pay and gender pension gaps), as well as being detrimental for the workforce and economy as a whole. This issue is currently receiving considerable attention from the Government, to include the following:

- Parliamentary Women and Equalities Committee report which looked at menopause in the workplace.

- House of Commons "Menopause and the Workplace" survey of 23.02.22

At the time of writing, the government's first response has included accepting in full, part or principle at least 50% of the recommendations, to include pre-paid prescription certificates to reduce the cost of a year's worth of HRT to around two individual prescription charges, and the appointment of a Menopause Champion.

---

[13] The Menopause and Workplace report by the Fawcett Society: https://www.fawcettsociety.org.uk/menopauseandtheworkplace

Future legislative changes will no doubt continue to be sought and the general expectation must sensibly be for the number of menopausal people experiencing life-changing symptoms to reduce over time. Logic would dictate that as the government and employers develop and finesse their policies and approaches, the extent of menopause-related employment (and thus earning capacity) issues should reduce within and without family law cases.

Notwithstanding this, at the current time there remains a need for family lawyers to think about whether their client's menopausal symptoms are such that they should be raised in family law cases. Practitioners should, though, avoid giving their clients unrealistic expectations, be express and clear about the lack of case law in this regard.

In a financial remedy case, early steps will include identification of net assets, income and pension provision, and perhaps a preliminary view about which of the available orders (section 22 – 24B Matrimonial Causes Act 1973) are likely to be required and sought.

It may be helpful for lawyers to broadly consider at this early stage what impact a party's menopausal symptoms may potentially have on capital, income and pension orders. In the wider family press, there are calls from The Family Law Menopause Project[14] for the impact of menopause and client's ability to work to be properly taken into account where financial settlements are drawn up: more spousal maintenance and avoidance of a clean break in such cases.

The question of whether or not the law develops in this way remains to be seen, though the writer would suggest it is unlikely given the trend in recent years towards reduced spousal maintenance, attempts

14 https://www.familylawpartners.co.uk/blog/divorce-and-menopause-poverty-trap

to have the Divorce (Financial Provision) Bill passed, and the recent debates within the House of Lords about reform of matrimonial finance law[15]. The writer would stress, again, that at the time of writing there is no family law menopause case law.

From a broad point of view, the following seems conceivable:

- Property /capital: Symptoms of anxiety could impact on, or drive, a wish to retain the family home almost at any cost and potentially at the expense of future pension income via offsetting. Practitioners should be wary of this and ensure that clients consult financial advisors as appropriate.

- Re pension provision: financial remedy matters only consider sharing of the pension provision in existence at the time of the proceedings. Even if that is shared to equalise the income it will yield for each party in retirement, disparity between the parties' future earning capacities (for example because of menopausal symptoms) are likely to result in disparities in terms of future pension accrual. Parties are ultimately likely to have different pension incomes in retirement. In this way, the impact of adverse menopausal symptoms may be felt financially in the future. It may be sensible for the client to specifically consider this scenario with their financial advisor, particularly if they are considering offsetting as above.

  Separately, even if the client is not considering offsetting and/or not facing a particular difference in future pension contributions, it is conceivable that menopausal symptoms could cause clients to agree financially detrimental outcomes

[15] https://hansard.parliament.uk/Lords/2023-03-08/debates/3AB3D708-24E5-4FF2-8481-05EFA27E2593/DivorceFinancialProvision

with regard to pension sharing generally. Where practitioner considers this is an issue, there will be a need for extremely clear, express file notes recording that they have identified this (perhaps with reference to symptoms, rather than with the 'menopause label') and in serious cases use a disclaimer.

- With regard to income, case law is clear that there is no presumption of sharing future income after divorce[16]. Menopausal symptoms will only begin to be relevant to income claims if they give rise to clear, identifiable and evidence supported need but there is no specific case law here and clients need to be aware of general trends in this area.

Section 25 factors

Delving deeper in the financial remedy matter, application of the pertinent section 25 factors is fundamental.

Section 25 (2) (a) Matrimonial Causes Act 1973

This legislation imposes a duty on the court exercising powers to make financial remedy orders to have particular regard to:

> "...the income, earning capacity, property and other financial resources which each of the parties to the matter has or is likely to have in the foreseeable future, including in the case of earning capacity any increase in that capacity which it would in the opinion of the court be reasonable to expect a party to the marriage to take steps to acquire..."

[16] Waggott v Waggott 2018 EWCA Civ 727; O'Dwyer v O'Dwyer [2019] EWHC 1838 (Fam)

It is beyond the remit of this book to examine whether or not this section of the legislation should be specifically changed or expanded to encompass the possibility that a party's earning capacity could reasonably decrease (by virtue of the menopause or anything else).

Practitioners and the court may therefore need to consider whether or not the asset profile has already been impacted by the menopause – for example, have menopausal symptoms adversely impacted either party's earning capacity (and if so the size of their pension pot in particular)?

A conclusive answer is likely to evade most practitioners not least because detailed, personal information about whether or not either party has started to experience menopausal symptoms would be required for any degree of accuracy. If you are not advising and representing the relevant party then this information may be difficult to come by, particularly if the parties have not had a close relationship for a number of years.

If acting for the menopausal party who would appear to have already experienced adverse symptoms of relevance, it is suggested that instructions should be taken to understand the following about your client:

- Their base line income prior to the menopause and whether or not that was also their maximum earning capacity;

- Since when they have been experiencing adverse menopausal symptoms;

- How their type of work, hours of work and remuneration for work have changed since the onset of menopausal symptoms;

- Whether or not they have an informed idea about for how much longer their menopausal symptoms might be influential.

- Whether there are reported cases which show how the court has dealt with other medium- long term symptoms which reduce earning capacity.

Not only could this be important in terms of framing your client's own case, but it may also be helpful information that could be needed to respond to enquiries and argument from the other party.

In the absence of case law relating to the menopause specifically, lawyers may need to identify and rely on cases where the court has considered other but similar symptoms.

Where it is deemed that the menopause has made no difference to the asset profile yet, thought may need to be given to whether this could be a possibility in the "foreseeable future". What is "...the foreseeable future..." will differ on a case-by-case basis. Arguably where a party is within 10 years of 'average' menopause age the foreseeable future could or should be interpreted as meaning until the end of their menopause. Again, there is no case law here.

Section 25 (2) (b) Matrimonial Causes Act 1973

The next factor requires particular regard to be given to:

> "...the financial needs, obligations and responsibilities which each of the parties to the marriage has or is likely to have in the foreseeable future..."

It is difficult to envisage circumstances where the menopause is likely to give rise to additional obligations or responsibilities for either party, so only the financial need aspect of this factor is examined here. In this regard, menopause could conceivably impact on financial need in the following ways:

(1) by virtue of the relevant party experiencing a reduced earning capacity during their menopausal years (note the cross over with section 25 (2)(a) here) and

(2) the menopausal party's expenditure needs significantly increasing because of, for example, the cost of a different diet, private GP fees and HRT prescriptions. Additionally, it could be the case that the menopausal party's general costs of living may increase by virtue of increased energy costs to support:

- Temperature control (e.g. air conditioning);
- More frequent use of washing machines/tumble dryers for larger amounts of laundry;
- Fuel, to travel to/from appointments;
- Increased consumption of painkillers;
- Increased need for clothing spanning a range of different sizes;
- Different skin care products and toiletries (for example, to treat skin/comfort complaints).

These costs could be significant and if so, should not be ignored.

A reduced earning capacity and/or deficit between expenditure needs and earned income is often dealt with by way of spousal maintenance. As already noted, at the time of writing, there is a trend within case law away from substantive, long term (or even joint lives orders) and towards much lower amounts of maintenance for shorter periods of time[17]. It may, or may not be, that the case of C v C (Financial Relief: Short Marriage) [1997] could be helpfully used, which states (page 43):

> "...the question is, can she adjust, not should she adjust..."

The case of C v C did not involve menopausal parties, however, it may be that this case could be used in support of an argument for spousal maintenance for a menopausal party subject to it being possible to provide evidence that the party cannot adjust.

Where periodical payments are appropriate, Section 25A Matrimonial Causes Act 1973 must be considered which provides that:-

> "(1) Where.....the court decides to exercise its powers...above in favour of a party to the marriage, it shall be the duty of the court to consider whether it would be appropriate so to exercise those powers that the financial obligations of each party towards the other will be terminated as soon after the grant of the decree as the court considers just and reasonable.
>
> (2) Where the court decides....to make a periodical payments...order in favour of a party to the marriage, the court shall in particular consider whether it would be appropriate to require those payments to be made...only for such term as would in the opinion of the court be sufficient to enable the party in whose favour the order is made to adjust without undue hardship to the termination of his or her financial dependence on the other party."

---

17 SS v NS [2014] EWHC 4183 (Fam); *A v M* [2021] EWFC 89.

The statutory steer towards a clean break as soon as possible is generally thought unhelpful and possibly detrimental to menopausal clients. Advice needs to be given about this, again being clear about prospects. Query whether future case law may provide guidance about the extent to which menopausal symptoms may impact on undue hardship.

Section 25 (2) (c) Matrimonial Causes Act 1973

> "...the standard of living enjoyed by the family before the breakdown of the marriage..."

With regard having already been given to the level of income and expenditure in the relationship, there is a risk of the 'standard of living' factor giving rise to some duplication.

There is a lot of information in the public domain about how adverse menopause symptoms may reduce a person's quality of life. The writer would suggest that this is different to menopausal symptoms impacting a person's standard of living, which might happen if the symptoms reduce their earning capacity for a period of time. This may particularly be the case in matters where expenditure needs already exceed income even before the menopause. As such, it is suggested that in such cases consideration and argument about whether the pre- or post-menopausal standard of living is the yardstick is unlikely to be an appropriate or affordable use of either party's legal fees.

Flowing from this, it would also seem logical that standard of living could very well impact on how menopausal symptoms are experienced and addressed.

As above, the onset or continuance of menopausal symptoms could increase a party's outgoings. It could be argued that the standard of living should guide the extent to which some of the additional outgoings could and should be factored into the matter. For example, where the family has previously paid privately for medical consultations etc, it is suggested it would not be unreasonable to argue that factoring in private menopause GP fees, and private prescriptions, is representative of the standard of living. The cost of private menopause GP consultations may be justifiable regardless of whether the party is already experiencing adverse symptoms.

Indeed, it may be that in higher income cases, menopausal clients are already receiving such treatment, that their symptoms are properly managed and thus would not be argued as relevant to the financial remedy case in any event.

Section 25 (2) (d) Matrimonial Causes Act 1973

> *"...the age of each party to the marriage and the duration of the marriage..."*

The age of a party may be a guide when considering whether the menopause is likely to be a factor in a case. NHS advice[18] is that the hormonal changes which prompt menopausal symptoms usually happen between the ages of 45 and 55. Practitioners should be aware it is only a guide, however. Menopause can naturally occur outside of this range. In addition, certain medical treatments which remove/impact on hormone producing organs (e.g. ovaries, uterus), certain cancer treatments, and other interventions can all prompt an early menopause.

There is plenty of case law examining how to calculate the duration of a marriage and how the duration of the marriage should impact on the financial provision to be made. For example, generally speaking, the

[18] https://www.nhs.uk/conditions/menopause/

longer the marriage the smaller the likely departure from an equal division of capital and pension assets.

Depending upon the age at which the parties were married, it is entirely possible that the need to consider menopausal matters increases with the duration of the marriage. There will be some anomalous cases, for example second marriages including a party who is already within their perimenopause, where the relevance of menopausal matters could decrease with the duration of marriage.

As with all the factors, in the absence of menopause specific case law, the next best thing at this time is to research cases in which the court has considered the particular symptoms being experienced.

Section 25 (2) (e) Matrimonial Causes Act 1973

> "...any physical or mental disability of either of the parties to the marriage..."

Again, for the avoidance of doubt, it is not suggested that people suffering from menopausal symptoms are disabled. The Equality Act 2010, section 6 (1) provides that:

> "A person (P) has a disability if –
>
> (a) P has a physical or mental impairment, **and**
>
> (b) the impairment has a substantial and long-term adverse effect on P's ability to carry out normal day-to-day activities"

Whilst the menopause itself is not a disability, employment courts and tribunals have found that some severe menopausal symptoms can be classified as disabilities[19].

It remains to be seen whether or not the family court will follow suit in this line of thinking. Again, there are no reported family law cases in which the menopause has been mentioned as a s25 disability. Instead, practitioners will find themselves reverting to 'general' financial remedy case law addressing how the court has dealt with certain disabilities[20].

That approach could lead practitioners to look at whether or not their client (or the other party) is experiencing symptoms which amount to "impairment". The court considered the matter of impairment in J v DLA Piper UK LLP UKEAT/0263/09 and commented that in most cases it will follow as a matter of common-sense inference that there is an impairment where it has been first established that there is a long-term substantial adverse effect on day-to-day activities.

Section25 (2) (f) Matrimonial Causes Act 1973

> "...the contributions which each of the parties has made or is likely in the foreseeable future to make to the welfare of the

---

19 Rooney v Leicester City Council; Daley v Optiva [2020] and Davies Scottish Courts and Tribunals Service [2018]

20 HC v FW [2017] EWHC 3162 (Fam); ND v GD [2021] needs do not need to be relationship generated; Miller v Miller; McFarlane v McFarlane 2006 (para 11 re needs); M v M (property adjustment: impaired life expectancy) *[1993] 2 FLR 723, CA. Seaton v Seaton [1986] 2 FLR 398, CA* and *Ashley v Blackman [1988] 2 FLR 278; [2015] EWHC 1670 (Fam), [2015] Fam Law 883, [2015] All ER (D) 163 (Jun).*

> family, including any contribution by looking after the home or caring for the family..."

Practitioners dealing with menopause cases should be aware of the care burdens their clients are likely to be facing in the foreseeable future.

The combination of increases in average age of marriage, childbirth, life expectancy (and thus years in ill health) now mean that albeit contributions to the care of children of the family may be reducing/almost irrelevant by the menopause window it now statistically likely that such care obligations may be replaced by the burden of caring for adult relatives[21].

The Matrimonial Causes Act 1973 specifically refers to caring for *the family*. The "family" is not defined in the act but the case law has generally taken this to mean the parties, children of both parties and any other child treated as though a child of both parties. As such,

---

21 According to the ONS the standardised mean age of a mother has increased by 9 years for women born in 1949 and those in 1975. From 22 to almost 31. According to the ONS for opposite sex divorces in 2021 the median duration of marriage at divorce was 12.3 years.

Again, according to the ONS marriage rates have generally been decreasing among younger age groups and increasing at older age groups. In 1975, the average age for a woman to marry was 26, and a man 29. These average ages have now increased to 35 and 38 respectively.

Again, ONS, people in the 50s and 60s are most likely to provide informal care to their parents or grandparents. Average life expectancy for someone born in 1980 was 70/76 male/female and is now 79/83. Healthy life expectancy is about 45% from age 65 (8/9 years in poor health)

practitioners should expressly address with their clients that the foreseeable future contributions made to the care of older generations will not be taken into account in terms of the law. This is a practical, not legal, problem which they will face. Practitioners should refer such clients to an independent financial advisor at an early stage so that appropriate financial advice, probably including cash flow planning, can be obtained and undertaken. As seems to be the theme, there are no reported cases which address the issue of caring for an adult relative in the section 25 context. The Family Justice Council guidance[22] makes the point about needs being the consequence of the parties' relationship. Arguably, a person's own elderly relatives and the need to care for them does not relate to the relationship in question at all, though caring for the other party's elderly relatives might.

The purpose of this textbook is not to consider the rights and wrongs of the current law. For the purposes of this book it must be accepted as fact that the care obligations of many menopausal clients (and others) are very likely to give rise to a gender pay gap[23] and gender pension gap. It is important for practitioners to alert clients to that and put them in touch with financial advisers to avoid clients later feeling the financial outcome did not adequately meet their needs and (probably wrongly) that this was because of some fault of the practitioner.

Again, full and frank acknowledgement of the fact that the current law could lead to what may be perceived as inequitable results is vital. A divorce is not an opportunity to change the law and most clients would not have the stomach to appeal and attempt to make new case

---

22 Family Justice Council Guidance on "Financial Needs" on Divorce: https://www.judiciary.uk/wp-content/uploads/2013/04/guidance-on-financial-needs-on-divorce-june-2016-2.pdf

23 UK gender pay gap – GOV.UK (www.gov.uk); Menopause and the Workplace inquiry

law. Divorce often presents a very real need for a person to undertake a financial review of their current and future circumstances in a way they may not have done before.

Section25 (2) (g) Matrimonial Causes Act 1973

> "...the conduct of each of the parties, if that conduct is such that it would in the opinion of the court be inequitable to disregard..."

It is suggested that this is not connected with the menopause, and thus not further considered here.

Section 25 (2) (h) Matrimonial Causes Act 1973

> "...the value to each of the parties to the marriage of the benefit which...that party will lose the chance of acquiring..."

Generally speaking the asset which often falls to be considered pursuant to this factor is pension provision. Pension sharing orders are generally used to deal with this. As outlined above, there is likely to be a pension gap between menopausal clients and their spouses, it is clear that there is no entitlement to sharing future income, and offsetting is possibly a greater risk. Financial advice is key.

Query the likelihood of successfully arguing that expenditure budgets should include future pension saving, given the case law with regard sharing income.

Creative application of case law

In the absence of specific menopause case law, in some ways family law practitioners may consider themselves to be in the invidious position of needing to apply other case law to these cases. In the alternative, the view could be taken that menopausal symptoms are a collection of issues which have (probably individually) arisen in other cases about which there is case law. As such a different approach could be to identify the relevant symptoms in your case and apply case law accordingly, for example:

Symptom	**Case law**
Changes to mood: low mood, anxiety, mood swings, low self-esteem;	In the case of RC v JC [2020] EWHC 466 (Fam) significant evidence was given about the wife's vulnerability to anxiety symptoms at times of stress, and her development of an anxiety disorder with depression. Evidence was given, in percentage terms, as to wife's improvement and prospects of recovery. The case was complex but ultimately the Judge decided not to ascribe an earning capacity to the wife.

Menopause can contribute to adverse financial outcomes

Once the foundation of financial information is in place, negotiations follow. Menopause symptoms, such as anxiety and stress, and lack of confidence, could all contribute to women agreeing potentially detrimental financial terms. For example, yearning for the legal process to be concluded very quickly, and/or absorbing a former partner's assertions about what they consider fair, could lead to women accepting less than their true entitlement. We particularly see this in relation to pensions.

Financial outcomes tend to be set in stone

This process cannot, generally, be revisited. Once agreed, outcomes tend to be final and binding, so it's incredibly important that, depending upon the available assets, the outcome is sufficient to meet housing and income needs now and for the future.

Again, strong legal support combined with independent financial advice, is vital.

CHAPTER FIVE

NUPTIAL AGREEMENTS

Practitioners are undertaking more nuptial agreement work now than ever before. In addition to all the basic advice and considerations (most of which is beyond the remit of this text) specific thought should be given to whether or not the menopause may be relevant at the time of drafting, or potential implementation of the agreement. In some instances it may be that particular menopause-related provision ought to be made.

Circumstances when agreeing the document

Family lawyers will be familiar with the basic requirements that need to be met for a nuptial agreement to be as strong as is possible according to current law.

The Radmacher[24] guidance and/or Law Commission recommend-dations[25] each require the parties to have entered into the relevant agreement freely. Consideration must be given to whether or not the parties are on an equal footing. Each case is of course fact specific but if either party is experiencing significant, adverse menopausal symptoms when the agreement is being negotiated then arguably that person may be at risk of significant disadvantage. Depending on the case, it may be that consideration should be given to how to mitigate

24 Radmacher v Granatino [2010] UKSC 42

25 https://s3-eu-west-2.amazonaws.com/lawcom-prod-storage-11jsxou24uy7q/uploads/2015/03/lc343_matrimonial_property.pdf

this risk through a range of measures. These might range from deliberately extending the timescale for negotiations, recording each party's health/life stage within the agreement, and particularly addressing and recording each party's emotional state at the time of making the agreement. In some cases it may be sensible to obtain a short medical report or blood test results. For those clients who would prefer not to consider, obtain or include detail such as this, family lawyers will want to ensure that they have specifically considered the issues, retained full file notes and advised the client about any potential detriment of agreeing terms whilst/if vulnerable. This might include possible difficulty arguing that the document should not be upheld at a later date on the basis of a party experiencing adverse menopausal symptoms whilst negotiating.

Additionally, parties must each have a full appreciation of the implications of the agreement. Again, with the potential adverse impact of menopausal symptoms in mind (particularly with reference to cognitive processing and other mental symptoms) it will be particularly important for a solicitor representing a client who may be within the perimenopause to take (and record) relevant instructions about that client's personal circumstances. This should ensure that any possible 'red flags', about their client's ability to retain and process complicated legal advice, are picked up. If this is a relevant issue, the practitioner will then want to utilise a variety of ways of conveying advice. This is particularly pertinent, with the content of the solicitor's certificate in mind (usually including confirmation that the solicitor believes their client has understood the legal advice given).

Content

Assuming any particular nuptial agreement adheres to the Radmacher guidance and/or Law Commission recommendations, the issue of whether or not it will be upheld ultimately comes down to whether or not the outcome is within the range of fairness. Assets allowing, this will require the agreement to meet the reasonable needs of each party and/or avoid an outcome leaving one party in a financial predicament with the other in a position of sufficiency or even surplus.

As acknowledged earlier within this publication, the menopause can significantly change (a) a person's financial needs and (b) a person's earning capacity/ability to meet their own financial needs. Family lawyers will want to raise, consider and advise about this during the negotiating and drafting process to ensure their clients are aware of how these issues might be relevant to the provision which should be made for them in the event of, and depending upon the timing of any permanent breakdown of the relationship.

From a wider perspective, this is also connected to reported gender pay and pension gaps. Specific consideration of those concepts is beyond the remit of this text, save to mention that where a relationship permanently breaks down at the time of, or after, one of the party's menopause it is increasingly likely that there will need to be a greater focus on that person's pension provision which might lead to a need for more pension sharing, among other orders.

CHAPTER SIX

CHILDREN ACT 1989 MATTERS

It is only recently that practitioners have started to actively consider how menopausal symptoms could be relevant to and impact on financial matters. The path is equally untrodden with regard to Children Act matters. Arguably, such matters involve considerably more qualitative analysis of issues of which menopausal symptoms might be just one.

Family law practitioners will all be fully conversant with section 8 Children Act 1989 which defines the orders that the court can make, as follows:

> "an order regulating arrangements relating to any of the following—
>
> (a) with whom a child is to live, spend time or otherwise have contact, and
>
> (b) when a child is to live, spend time or otherwise have contact with any person;
>
> "a prohibited steps order" means an order that no step which could be taken by a parent in meeting his parental responsibility for a child, and which is of a kind specified in the order, shall be taken by any person without the consent of the court;
>
> "a specific issue order" means an order giving directions for the purpose of determining a specific question which has arisen, or

> which may arise, in connection with any aspect of parental responsibility for a child."

Against a backdrop of the child's welfare being the paramount consideration, the factors to which the court shall have particular regard when making decisions about children, which are set out at section 1(3) Children Act 1989 are:

> "(a) the ascertainable wishes and feelings of the child concerned (considered in the light of his age and understanding);
>
> (b) his physical, emotional and educational needs;
>
> (c) the likely effect on him of any change in his circumstances;
>
> (d) his age, sex, background and any characteristics of his which the court considers relevant;
>
> (e) any harm which he has suffered or is at risk of suffering;
>
> (f) how capable each of his parents, and any other person in relation to whom the court considers the question to be relevant, is of meeting his needs;
>
> (g) the range of powers available to the court under this Act in the proceedings in question."

This is not a conclusive list so the first point to make is that there is nothing in law to say that the court cannot take into account the menopausal status of either or both parents, in addition or separately to the welfare checklist.

Returning to the welfare checklist, however, family lawyers will likely be drawn to 1(3)(f) as being a factor where the question/fact of menopause could be of most relevance. It is all too common for parties to (mis)interpret differences in parenting style and view it as the other parent being incapable, or less capable, of meeting their child's needs. It does seem plausible, however, that menopausal symptoms could have an impact on a person's usual or basic parenting style. The below table gives some potential examples:

Symptom	**<u>Potential</u> impact on parenting style/parenting capability**
Sleep interruption	Short temper, change in decisions made. Reduced patience.
Mood swings	Less consistent parenting, less consistency in day-to-day situations.
Fatigue	Reduction in energy to play with and meet physical demands of children.
Decline in mental health: Depressed mood, anxious mood, problems with memory or concentration (including brain fog)	Difficulties balancing all demands of daily life. Reduction in guidance and support provided to children. Potentially reduced social interaction for children, which could include children not being taken to school as required, not being supported with homework and not having key equipment/clothing etc Increased likelihood of children suffering from depression in the future

Significant headaches/migraines	Temporary inability to engage/care for children (lasting hours – days)

It is very important to note that it is not suggested that all menopausal people will (a) experience these symptoms and/or (b) be impacted on a worst-case scenario basis. Practitioners should, however, keep the issues in mind. It is not for practitioners or their clients to diagnose the symptoms but if allegations of the above nature are made in any particular case it may be appropriate for the lawyer advising the subject party to consult their GP. Again, at the time of writing there is no case law which might provide authority for any particular menopause related approach but thought might also be given to seeking an order for a s7 CAFCASS report with the specific requirement that CAFCASS consider how menopausal symptoms may be relevant to the allegations and issues.

From another perspective, were a party to be experiencing the above symptoms it is possible/likely that this could impact how a child feels about either parent or their life with either parent and thus their ascertainable wishes and feelings **1(3)(a)**. Children are not expected to make their own decisions about their time/living arrangements but if their feelings are being coloured by a party's menopausal symptoms practitioners should consider how that could be addressed if at all. It is acknowledged that this may fall within the family lawyer's remit to signpost their clients to other appropriate resources, since changes/improvements to a parent/child relationship are plainly not legal matters.

In very extreme cases it is possible that a parent's adverse menopausal symptoms could put their child(ren) at risk of harm **1(3)(e)**, particularly if that parent finds that they are unable to look after themselves or if they experienced (and/or acted on) suicidal thoughts. In such circumstances the practitioner will need to consider the safety and welfare issues very carefully to include making a report to the local authority children's services department if their client does or will not.

CHAPTER SEVEN

DOMESTIC ABUSE & FAMILY LAW ACT APPLICATIONS

When relationships break down, there are occasions when it becomes too difficult for the parties to remain living together. If necessary, applications can be made for orders regulating occupation of the house, excluding one party from the house entirely, and/or preventing the parties from molesting one another.

These types of orders usually require the court to find inter parties' abuse and, importantly, to consider the impact of the abuse on the parties. In this regard, the balance of harm test at s33(7) Family Law Act 1996 applies as follows:

> "if it appears to the court that the applicant or any relevant child is likely to suffer significant harm attributable to conduct of the respondent if an order under this section… is not made, the court shall make the order unless it appears to it that –
>
> (a) the respondent or any relevant child is likely to suffer significant harm if the order is made; and
>
> (b) the harm likely to be suffered by the respondent or child in that event is as great as, or greater than, the harm attributable to conduct of the respondent which is likely to be suffered by the applicant or child if the order is not made"

It is entirely possible that the extent to which a party is suffering from menopausal symptoms could influence whether and/or how much harm they may suffer as a result of the other's conduct. For example. a person whose mental health is already somewhat reduced because of adverse menopause symptoms may be particularly sensitive to conduct which they might otherwise feel able to endure or deal with.

As such, there *may* be an increased risk of harm to parties suffering from the menopause which might either increase their chances of obtaining an occupation order, or increase their chances of being able to resist such (depending on whether they are applicant or respondent in the proceedings).

In relation to non-molestation orders, which the court can make under section 42 Family Law Act 1996, the well-being of the applicant is a circumstance to which the court shall have regard per section 42(5) Family Law Act 1996 as follows:

> "In deciding whether to exercise its powers under this section and, if so, in what manner, the court shall have regard to all the circumstances including the need to secure the health, safety and well-being of (a) the applicant and (b) of any relevant child."

Family Procedure Rules

FPR2010 3A and the associated practice direction are particularly pertinent. At 3A., they set out how, inter alia, the court must have regard to (with the writer's emphasis):

(a) **the impact** of any action or **perceived** intimidation, including any behaviour towards the party or witness on the part of:

(i) any other party or other witness to the proceedings… or

(ii) any members of the family of the party or witnesses

(b) **whether the party** or witnesses:

(i) **suffer from mental disorder** or otherwise have a significant impairment of intelligence or social functioning;

(ii) have a physical disability or suffer from a physical disorder; or

(iii) **are undergoing medical treatment**

and

(k) **whether any measure is available to the court**

At this point, the practitioner may wish to pause to consider whether or not a party receiving HRT, medication to regulate menopause related mood difficulties, talking therapy and so on, might be said to be undergoing medical treatment.

In respect of the measures that the court might take, the FPR sets out at 3A.8 (again, with the writer's emphasis) that the court may:

(b) **allow a party…**to participate in hearings and give evidence by live link;

and

(d) **provide for a party…to participate in proceedings with the assistance of an intermediary;**

and

(f) **do anything else which is set out in PD 3AA**

Such measures may be helpful or required if a menopausal party may struggle to understand or answer questions under pressure because of, for example, brain fog or anxiety. Also, arguably it may be more important that these measures are taken where a menopausal party is unrepresented though, from a practical perspective, it is foreseeable that without a legal representative that party is probably unlikely to be aware of any potential relevance of the menopause to their case.

Additionally, particularly until there is any case law giving clear guidance in this regard, practitioners may again find themselves thinking about what other (non-menopause specific) case law could arguably be applicable. For example, there is case law detailing measures to be taken in cases involving parties with other vulnerabilities (for example, learning disabilities) and these could be helpful in menopause cases. The simplified judgment attached to the full judgment as in *A Local Authority v G (Parent with learning disability [2017] EWFC B94* is one such example.

Coercion and control

In recent years, at a grassroots level in family law matters, the writer would suggest there has been a definite increase in the number of cases involving allegations of one party's controlling and coercive behaviour against the other.

The criminal offence of controlling or coercive behaviour in intimate or familial relationships[26] defines those behaviour types with reference

[26] Serious Crimes Act 2015 as amended by DAA 2021

to the perpetrator's wish to make a person subordinate and/or harmful, punishing and frightening behaviour.

As family law starts to get to grips with the menopause, it will be interesting to see whether or not there is any connection between menopausal symptoms and (a) potential vulnerability to being a victim of controlling and coercive behaviour or (b) being a potential perpetrator of such behaviour.

Narcissism

Again, over the last few years, the family law press has increasingly featured articles and publications about narcissism. The message from those texts is that this is another issue about which we need to be aware, and which could give rise to a very particular approach to cases. It may be that this is another area where we might start to see texts considering the inter-relationship with menopause.

CHAPTER EIGHT

COHABITATION MATTERS

Cohabitation agreements are really contracts between people planning to, or already, living together. Lawyers will keep in mind the key requirements for an enforceable contract (offer, acceptance, consideration, intention to create legal relationship and certainty of terms) but this is beyond the remit of this text and it is not suggested there is any particular connection with the menopause here.

The writer would suggest that practitioners representing a cohabitant client who may not have, or only have a very small, beneficial interest in the proposed home will routinely take time to consider with such clients how they would meet their housing need if the relationship broke down. Lawyers may think it appropriate to take that discussion one step further to look at how the menopause generally, and separately any adverse menopausal symptoms, may impact on a practical level.

On the current law, the breakdown of a cohabitating relationship will be governed by contract law (in relation to any cohabitation agreement), land and trust law (in relation to any disputes about ownership of the property). Cohabitants do not currently have the benefit of a judge being able to exercise discretion or make decisions based on a broad concept of "fairness". As such, if they consider it fair for particular provision to be made so that they can meet needs if a relationship breaks down either when they have already fallen into a gender pay gap, or at a time when their earning (and thus mortgage) capacity may be insufficient then they need to address and negotiate that as a term of a contract.

Clearly, parties who are not married or in a civil partnership will not be able to obtain pension sharing orders. In certain cases consideration may need to be given to seeking agreement for a particular cash lump sum, although it is acknowledged that such cases are likely to be few and far between.

Whilst cohabitation agreements are generally negotiated at the start of the cohabiting relationship, practitioners should consider advising clients to review and renegotiate them at key points which might include the menopause. Drafting review provisions of this nature into the agreement at the start will likely increase the chances of reviews taking place.

CHAPTER NINE

DISABILITY, PROTECTED CHARACTERISTICS, ETHNIC MINORITIES, ETHNIC GROUPS AND LGBTQ+

The government reports which have been published have recognised that the majority of menopause awareness information specifically relates to white, middleclass women. It would seem that most research and attention in this area has focused on professional or managerial, white, middle-class, able-bodied women.

The reports have looked at issues including how different ethnic groups experience menopausal symptoms at different ages, over different time periods and with difference in symptoms. At the current time ethnic minority, disabled, and LGBTQ+ people may feel and/or experience more stigma around the menopause[27] than their white, able-bodied counterparts. The writer would suggest that, at present, these reports are not necessarily a resource to which one might direct a client, but that they are an important and informative read for

27 Women and Equalities Committee: Menopause and the workplace Report 28.07.22 – https://publications.parliament.uk/pa/cm5803/cmselect/cmwomeq/91/summary.html which quoted UNISON, TUC, Business in the Community and the International Menopause/Work Consortium

anyone representing a non-white, non-middleclass, person going through the menopause.

A clear take-away from the reports is the willingness (or not) of people from different minority backgrounds and the LGBTQ+ community, to speak about the menopause, and how this differs widely. This may impact on the ease with which the family law practitioner identifies and approaches discussion about the menopause for such clients and thus be something about which the family lawyer will want to be aware. What is certainly common to all clients is the need for appropriate sensitivity, and to take your lead from the client.

CHAPTER TEN

EVIDENCE AND EXPERTS

It will be clear from earlier chapters that the writer en visages that there will be occasions when family lawyers will want to consider obtaining and adducing expert evidence relating to the menopause.

It is not suggested that this will be required in anywhere near every case. Certainly, a need for menopause evidence or experts is only likely to arise in cases where a client and/or their lawyer has identified menopausal symptoms as being potentially so adverse and significant that they could impact on the case outcome.

The writer would suggest that where this is an issue, the family lawyer will first consider GP evidence before then obtaining any further expert evidence. It must, though, be noted that at the time of writing there is no key body of law or cases to confirm what type of expert evidence should be sought and what weight should be attached to it. General information can be obtained from the British Menopause Society Overview – British Menopause Society (thebms.org.uk) which society is endorsed by the NHS Menopause – Help and support – NHS (www.nhs.uk).

GP

Logically, where arguing that menopause is so relevant as to impact case outcome, basic evidence will be needed that the relevant party is indeed within the perimenopause. The client's own NHS GP might be the first port of call for many. This will require the client's doctor to use their professional knowledge and experience, for example to decide whether or not to order blood tests. Clients may wish to ask for such if they are not offered. To obtain evidence of this nature, clients may request such direct from their GP but it is suggested that a quicker and more economic approach may be for the client to register for full access to their medical records via the NHS app[28]. Depending on what the GP surgery shares it is likely that the client will then be able to provide their lawyer with instructions/copy records showing their medical history, consultation notes and test results.

It is understood that fluctuating hormone levels and thus the manifestation of symptoms can be so variable as to produce wildly different blood test results on different days. Additionally, blood test results in and of themselves may well require expert explanation particularly if they are to feature as evidence in a legal matter. The GP could be asked to produce a written narrative advice or explanation, but they may be unwilling to do so if this is not required for the patient's treatment and/or ordered to do so by the court. Other options might include a private GP not constrained by the demands and economies of the NHS, or services to which the client might have access through private medical cover.

Once evidence has been obtained that the client is within the perimenopause, the writer considers the next step will be to evidence the diagnosis (with regard to symptoms), treatment and prognosis.

---

28 https://www.nhs.uk/using-the-nhs/about-the-nhs/how-to-get-your-medical-records/

Again, the treating clinician will usually be best placed to do this outside of legal proceedings. Where this is required for a legal case, however, lawyers will be conscious that such evidence is usually treated with caution by the other party because of concerns about a doctor's bias towards their patient.

As is the theme, there is no case law to rely on yet. As a matter of common sense it is suggested that it is only where the treating clinician's evidence suggests that treatment is not working sufficiently well (i.e. the client continues to experience significant, detrimental symptoms on a day-to-day basis), or the prognosis for unmanageable/debilitating symptoms goes beyond short-term that further evidence or expert involvement is likely to be helpful. As such, the use of the treating clinician's evidence may arguably be limited to justifying the instruction of another specialist.

Further expert(s)

In cases where notwithstanding treatment (e.g. HRT) there is evidence of unmanageable/debilitating menopause symptoms, it might be helpful to consider obtaining further expert evidence. Before doing so careful thought should be given to the purpose of the evidence and what form it should take. Broadly, what is it hoped the evidence will show, or what is the purpose of the evidence?

Recent case law in other areas has focussed on the importance and requirement for any expert to be properly expert. As such, whilst there is an increasing array of private menopause specialists available to be consulted (both as to the medical side of things, as well as treatment of symptoms rather than cause) care should be taken to identify an appropriate expert with reference to the issue in the case. It may be that this is a practitioner who has a specialism in menopause but who also practises in other areas.

The following experts may be suitable (which list is not exhaustive):

Purpose of evidence	
Report about the likely timeframe of unmanageable/debilitating symptoms	Endocrinology report[29]
Report about impact of symptoms on the client's ability to perform usual occupation, limitations, mitigations	Occupational Therapist
Report about impact of symptoms on client's ability to care for the children	Independent Social Worker
Report about client's ability to take part in, and attend, court proceedings	Doctor (paragraph 36 *Levy v Ellis-Carr* *[2012] EWHC 63 (Ch)* refers)

In cases before the court, or within arbitration, a formal Part 25 application should be made. The practical question of how to do that is beyond the remit of this book but it is anticipated most practitioners will be very familiar with the procedure in any event.

29 https://www.endocrinology.org/endocrinologist/128-summer18/features/spotlight-on-menopause/

Parties' own evidence

In cases being resolved via arbitration or court proceedings, there is a very real possibility of each party needing to give verbal evidence. Previous chapters have highlighted how such a need may impact on mental symptoms, such as anxiety.

Clients may be concerned about how their physical symptoms may manifest themselves whilst giving evidence, and how this may affect their apparent credibility. In this regard, practitioners may wish to assure clients that whilst symptoms may give a party a certain demeanour or presentation, judges have to be very cautious not to make decisions about credibility solely on appearance and behaviour (e.g paragraph 36 *R (on the application of SS (Sri Lanka)) v Secretary of State for the Home Department [2018] EWCA Civ 1391).*

CHAPTER ELEVEN

SHOULD THE MENOPAUSE BE RUN AS AN ISSUE?

There may be multiple cases where the family lawyer has identified that a particular client is suffering from adverse menopausal symptoms. In some of these, it may also be identified that debilitating symptoms could sensibly form the basis of pleadings within the relevant family law matter. Even so, it is suggested that both practitioner and client will want to think very carefully before committing to raising and pursuing such an issue ("running a menopause case" or "menopause argument").

Even where a menopausal client is generally willing to make submissions about the adverse impact of symptoms, the writer would suggest that some form of cost benefit risk analysis should also be performed. Both emotional and financial costs might arise from running a menopause case, and the importance of each will vary between clients.

Considering potential emotional benefits and costs in the first instance. Family law practitioners frequently encounter clients who wish to provide detailed instructions about every aspect of their lives. At times it seems they cannot rest easy without so doing. Increasing recognition of and discussion about the menopause within society, the workplace and at a governmental level, may well give rise to larger numbers of clients volunteering this type information to their lawyer. Indeed, to an extent they may feel compelled to do so to ensure that they have not failed to mention something which could have been relevant to the outcome of their case. This may be perceived as a potential emotional benefit of client-lawyer discussions about menopausal symptoms, but the writer would suggest there is a significant difference between acknowledging and discussion issues at 'file level' as opposed to voicing and running arguments within the case itself. It is, in fact, difficult to easily identify potential emotional benefits of running a menopause argument. On the other hand, the writer would suggest that the potential emotional costs of running a menopause case are more clearly identifiable and perhaps even obvious.

By its very nature, running a menopause case will involve revealing personal information about the client to the other party involved, and their legal representatives, at the very least. In circumstances where there is a fairly high likelihood of the parties' relationship being somewhat strained, it would perhaps not be surprising if the client ultimately concluded that they would rather not disclose their menopausal symptoms to their former partner. For many, it is entirely foreseeable that an emotional cost benefit analysis will indicate against running an argument of this nature before the element of risk is even brought into consideration.

Turning, then, to potential financial benefits of proceeding in this way. As identified earlier in this book, in some cases it may indeed be possible to quantify and establish a causal connection between expenditure costs, reduced earning capacity and menopausal symptoms. The lawyer should be able to estimate (usually a range) by how much costs might increase if such issues are to be considered within a matter. For example, the lawyer can consider the costs of a Part 25 application, the costs of any relevant expert and so on and so forth.

Even where this financial information is available however, at the current time the absence of case law means it will be rare for a practitioner to be able to offer any meaningful advice or assurance about the prospects of the menopause argument succeeding. Consequently, until and unless case law changes, there is likely to be considerable risk associated with running cases of this nature.

All this may leave clients in some difficulty giving positive instructions to run a menopause case as an issue unless they feel extremely strongly or passionately about it, or in what are likely to be extremely rare cases clear, significant and substantial financial benefits are identifiable. As such, it may be that only those suffering from severely debilitating symptoms will feel minded to proceed at this time.

CHAPTER TWELVE

FAMILY LAWYERS AND THE MENOPAUSE

More than 50% of solicitors are female[30]. The percentage of female lawyers working in the family law area is significantly higher than that.

As such, more family lawyers than not are likely to experience menopausal symptoms at some point in their careers.

Managing menopausal symptoms whilst working

Again, it is known that working within the legal profession is stressful. As well as dealing with difficult legal issues, family lawyers also have to navigate and support their clients through complex emotional situations. The relationship between a lawyer's adverse menopausal symptoms and this subject matter will be complicated.

It is not suggested that female lawyers are unable to manage symptoms or to separate their personal lives from their work. However, where lawyers acknowledge and identify such difficulties there are practical ways to mitigate these, as follows:

---

[30] https://www.sra.org.uk/sra/equality-diversity/diversity-profession/diverse-legal-profession/ and www.lawsociety.org.uk/contact-or-visit-us/press-office/press-releases/number-of-solicitors-on-the-roll-reaches-record-high

Symptom	**Potential impact on practice**	**Ways to mitigate impact of symptoms on practice**
Sleep interruption / fatigue	Increased likelihood of errors, impaired thinking, general decline in mental health.	Focus on self-care and nourishment. Reduce attempts to burn the candle at both ends. Co-work on cases with colleagues. Carefully consider workloads and personal energy when agreeing deadlines. Introduce additional days as buffer.
Mood swings	Potentially less consistent in demeanour, approach, rapport with both clients and colleagues.	If possible, work from home during most difficult times.

Decline in mental health: Depressed mood, anxious mood, problems with memory or concentration (including brain fog)	Difficulties balancing all demands of daily life/work Potentially reduced enthusiasm to guidance and support clients and colleagues	Engage with a professional family law supervisor[31] or your firm's mental health first-aider.
Significant headaches/migraines	Temporary inability to engage or work.	Engage with GP/menopause specialist in relation to medical aspects.
Hot flushes	Embarrassment in public	If possible work from home or ask for improved temperature control in the office.

[31] https://www.familylawsupervisors.co.uk/full-register-of-supervisors/

Minimising potential loss of talent

To the extent that those symptoms are more than fleeting, mild or 'a nuisance' this also means that the family law profession is more vulnerable than many to the risk of practitioners leaving the profession during/following the menopause.

Partners and those in managerial positions should consider this issue carefully and take steps to reduce the risk as far as possible. This may include the introduction of:

- Menopause champions – people who are specifically trained in how to support those going through the perimenopause;

- A specific Menopause Policy, to educate and provide information and guidance about supporting and empowering people transitioning through the menopause at work to feel confident to discuss it, to seek support and reasonable adjustments;

- Perhaps the signing of a pledge, such as the "Wellbeing of Women's Menopause Workplace pledge"

CHAPTER THIRTEEN

AVOIDING POTENTIAL NEGLIGENCE

The sudden increase of information and awareness of menopausal symptoms in the absence of any directly applicable case law could lead to a, hopefully temporary, period where there is a higher risk of professional negligence due to lack of guidance.

To avoid this, it is important that practitioners purposefully and actively consider how menopause may impact in each and every case, and make a full and written record to evidence that by:

1. Always considering comfort and logistics of meetings;
2. Asking appropriate, sensitively framed questions about symptoms within or before the initial consultation;
3. Not going beyond your remit as a lawyer: referring clients to others to provide symptomatic or general menopause support and treatment as required
4. Actively considering the extent to which any client falls within the category or definition of 'vulnerable' and proceed according to professional rules;
5. Even where clients would not be classified as 'vulnerable' deliberately reduce verbose correspondence and provide advice in a variety of ways/formats;
6. Actively consider the suitability of the pathway for resolution with menopausal symptoms in mind

7. Seek expert evidence where necessary.

8. Support your team.

CONCLUSION

The difficulties which challenging menopausal symptoms can create extend far beyond family law matters. To a significant extent, the issues need to be, and are being, addressed at far higher than 'relationship' level. As the level of available help, support and treatment increases from the government and employers in particular, the less scope there is likely to be for family practitioners to need to consider this within the subject matter of any particular case.

There is a huge amount of information about the menopause in the public domain. At all times lawyers will need to ensure they stay on the right side of signposting clients to such advice, rather than providing medical, therapeutic or other non-legal advice.

It is right that when practitioners are meeting with, advising and representing their clients, they specifically consider any menopausal symptoms from which that client may be suffering. In terms of the family law case itself, such symptoms will invariably be just one of a number of competing factors that need to be considered. The writer would suggest that it will take a very unique and specific set of circumstances for menopausal symptoms to be such that they are particularly determinative as to the outcome of the matter.

On the other hand and in direct contrast, once on notice that their client is, or may be, suffering from challenging symptoms of the menopause it will be exceedingly important that in *every* such case the practitioner takes appropriate steps to address any potential vulnerability and to check satisfactory delivery, receipt and retention of advice. The need for this specific client care will continue to be critical regardless of any wider changes and improvements delivered by the legislature.

'A Practical Guide to Hoarding and Mental Health for Housing Lawyers' by Rachel Coyle
'A Practical Guide to Psychiatric Claims in Personal Injury – 2nd Edition' by Liam Ryan
'Stephens on Contractual Indemnities' by Richard Stephens
'A Practical Guide to the EU Succession Regulation' by Richard Frimston
'A Practical Guide to Solicitor and Client Costs – 2nd Edition' by Robin Dunne
'Constructive Dismissal – Practice Pointers and Principles' by Benjimin Burgher
'A Practical Guide to Religion and Belief Discrimination Claims in the Workplace' by Kashif Ali
'A Practical Guide to the Law of Medical Treatment Decisions' by Ben Troke
'Fundamental Dishonesty and QOCS in Personal Injury Proceedings: Law and Practice' by Jake Rowley
'A Practical Guide to the Law in Relation to School Exclusions' by Charlotte Hadfield & Alice de Coverley
'A Practical Guide to Divorce for the Silver Separators' by Karin Walker
'The Right to be Forgotten – The Law and Practical Issues' by Melissa Stock
'A Practical Guide to Planning Law and Rights of Way in National Parks, the Broads and AONBs' by James Maurici QC, James Neill et al
'A Practical Guide to Election Law' by Tom Tabori
'A Practical Guide to the Law in Relation to Surrogacy' by Andrew Powell
'A Practical Guide to Claims Arising from Fatal Accidents – 2nd Edition' by James Patience
'A Practical Guide to the Ownership of Employee Inventions – From Entitlement to Compensation' by James Tumbridge & Ashley Roughton
'A Practical Guide to Asbestos Claims' by Jonathan Owen & Gareth McAloon
'A Practical Guide to Stamp Duty Land Tax in England and Northern Ireland' by Suzanne O'Hara
'A Practical Guide to the Law of Farming Partnerships' by Philip Whitcomb
'Covid-19, Homeworking and the Law – The Essential Guide to Employment and GDPR Issues' by Forbes Solicitors
'Covid-19 and Criminal Law – The Essential Guide' by Ramya Nagesh
'Covid-19 and Family Law in England and Wales – The Essential Guide' by Safda Mahmood

'A Practical Guide to the Law of Unlawful Eviction and Harassment – 2nd Edition' by Stephanie Lovegrove
'Covid-19, Brexit and the Law of Commercial Leases – The Essential Guide' by Mark Shelton
'A Practical Guide to Costs in Personal Injury Claims – 2nd Edition' by Matthew Hoe
'A Practical Guide to the General Data Protection Regulation (GDPR) – 2nd Edition' by Keith Markham
'Ellis on Credit Hire – Sixth Edition' by Aidan Ellis & Tim Kevan
'A Practical Guide to Working with Litigants in Person and McKenzie Friends in Family Cases' by Stuart Barlow
'Protecting Unregistered Brands: A Practical Guide to the Law of Passing Off' by Lorna Brazell
'A Practical Guide to Secondary Liability and Joint Enterprise Post-Jogee' by Joanne Cecil & James Mehigan
'A Practical Guide to the Pre-Action RTA Claims Protocol for Personal Injury Lawyers' by Antonia Ford
'A Practical Guide to Neighbour Disputes and the Law' by Alexander Walsh
'A Practical Guide to Forfeiture of Leases' by Mark Shelton
'A Practical Guide to Coercive Control for Legal Practitioners and Victims' by Rachel Horman
'A Practical Guide to Rights Over Airspace and Subsoil' by Daniel Gatty
'Tackling Disclosure in the Criminal Courts – A Practitioner's Guide' by Narita Bahra QC & Don Ramble
'A Practical Guide to the Law of Driverless Cars – Second Edition' by Alex Glassbrook, Emma Northey & Scarlett Milligan
'A Practical Guide to TOLATA Claims' by Greg Williams
'A Practical Guide to Elderly Law – 2nd Edition' by Justin Patten
'A Practical Guide to Responding to Housing Disrepair and Unfitness Claims' by Iain Wightwick
'A Practical Guide to the Construction and Rectification of Wills and Trust Instruments' by Edward Hewitt
'A Practical Guide to the Law of Bullying and Harassment in the Workplace' by Philip Hyland
'How to Be a Freelance Solicitor: A Practical Guide to the SRA-Regulated Freelance Solicitor Model' by Paul Bennett

'A Practical Guide to Prison Injury Claims' by Malcolm Johnson
'A Practical Guide to the Small Claims Track - 2nd Edition' by Dominic Bright
'A Practical Guide to Advising Clients at the Police Station' by Colin Stephen McKeown-Beaumont
'A Practical Guide to Antisocial Behaviour Injunctions' by Iain Wightwick
'Practical Mediation: A Guide for Mediators, Advocates, Advisers, Lawyers, and Students in Civil, Commercial, Business, Property, Workplace, and Employment Cases' by Jonathan Dingle with John Sephton
'The Mini-Pupillage Workbook' by David Boyle
'A Practical Guide to Crofting Law' by Brian Inkster
'A Practical Guide to Spousal Maintenance' by Liz Cowell
'A Practical Guide to the Law of Domain Names and Cybersquatting' by Andrew Clemson
'A Practical Guide to the Law of Gender Pay Gap Reporting' by Harini Iyengar
'A Practical Guide to the Rights of Grandparents in Children Proceedings' by Stuart Barlow
'NHS Whistleblowing and the Law' by Joseph England
'Employment Law and the Gig Economy' by Nigel Mackay & Annie Powell
'A Practical Guide to Noise Induced Hearing Loss (NIHL) Claims' by Andrew Mckie, Ian Skeate, Gareth McAloon
'An Introduction to Beauty Negligence Claims – A Practical Guide for the Personal Injury Practitioner' by Greg Almond
'Intercompany Agreements for Transfer Pricing Compliance' by Paul Sutton
'Zen and the Art of Mediation' by Martin Plowman
'A Practical Guide to the SRA Principles, Individual and Law Firm Codes of Conduct 2019 – What Every Law Firm Needs to Know' by Paul Bennett
'A Practical Guide to Adoption for Family Lawyers' by Graham Pegg
'A Practical Guide to Industrial Disease Claims' by Andrew Mckie & Ian Skeate
'A Practical Guide to Redundancy' by Philip Hyland
'A Practical Guide to Vicarious Liability' by Mariel Irvine
'A Practical Guide to Applications for Landlord's Consent and Variation of Leases' by Mark Shelton
'A Practical Guide to Relief from Sanctions Post-Mitchell and Denton' by Peter Causton

www.ingramcontent.com/pod-product-compliance
Ingram Content Group UK Ltd.
Pitfield, Milton Keynes, MK11 3LW, UK
UKHW020150290926
15471UKWH00004B/792

9 781912 687633